My Good Friend Walt Disney

◆

Artin Allahverdi

authorHOUSE®

AuthorHouse™
1663 Liberty Drive
Bloomington, IN 47403
www.authorhouse.com
Phone: 1-800-839-8640

First published by AuthorHouse 11/2/2009

ISBN: 978-1-4490-4626-2 (e)
ISBN: 978-1-4490-4627-9 (sc)

Printed in the United States of America
Bloomington, Indiana

This book is printed on acid-free paper.

Dedication

I would like to decade these book to my grandfather Aram Allahverdi who when I was a kid he introduce me to Walt Disney. When I was young me and my grandfather watched a lot of Disney films and I was hooked for life and become a writer thanks to my grandfather and Walt Disney. My grandfather took the time to let me be who I want to be growing up and my grandfather is a part of who I am and I thanked him for that for introducing me to Walt Disney to set free my imagination.

Chapter One

— ◆ —

Growing up I really didn't have that many friends I could talk to so I kept to myself a lot all my family that knows me pretty well and my grandfather. A lot of kids made fun of me and that hurts my feelings but I got over it now it doesn't bug me anymore. One thing that changed my life for good is when I was two years old one every movie that changed my life for good.

When I was two years old my grandfather showed me my first Disney film that's called "Pinocchio" the second Disney film that have been made back in 1939. Both me and my grandfather watch that movie together and the both of us were really entertained one hundred percent something that my grandfather wont forget but I was pretty young so I don't remember.

To me that's something that I really treasure for the rest of my life that my grandfather introduced me to Walt Disney pictures that's something I will never forget. Walt Disney has that special magic that forever will have that magic that people will pass down to children's and to their own children no matter what generation.

I got a little older I started to watch The Disney Channel I started watching so many different Disney films that is still hooked to me and I'm twenty–seven. Even when I was a little boy I never made any friends cause I had a hard time but I feel like Walt Disney took me and be my very dear friend for now and forever.

Making friends with somebody like Walt Disney is a special kind of bond something that you will never forget growing up. Disney has that same kind of magic that you will never forget that people have that special bond for anybody like between me and my grandfather when I was young. I always treasurer my friendship between Disney and myself growing up.

Friendship between me and Walt Disney is a bond that will never been broken and never will cause because when I was a little boy me and my grandfather always enjoyed watching Disney movies together. The bond between me and Walt Disney is something that I will never forget because it brings people together to enjoy the life of the magic.

I feel like Disney is part of who I am cause Walt Disney has given me something to believe in myself something to reach for the star just like Walt Disney did. Cause it's always important to reach for a star like wishing upon a star because you should always stud up what you believe in and that's what Walt Disney showed me "Reach For A Star"

Walt Disney not only made me believe in myself he teach me about value always doing the right thing and don't care what other's think about you and friendship and honor. Those are values that I've never forgotten growing up that later on in life will come in handed and I thanked all to Walt Disney a wonderful adviser for somebody like me growing up looking up to him.

Knowing Walt Disney is a friendship part of my life I grown up to be a good responsible person knowing the deferent's between right from wrong. All of the movies and animations in the past Walt Disney has shown me and guided me thru life the deferent's going to the right path and not going to the wrong path.

Getting to know Walt Disney as he has so much imagination inside of his mind that people followed for future generations and which I've grown up looking up to Walt Disney. I feel like Walt Disney is my very best friend he took me in when I didn't had any friends growing up and I thanked him for that since he passed on and forever in the future.

Thanks to Walt Disney he let me set free on my imagination to become a writer and to be who I am to be on the inside I can't imagine my life without Walt Disney in it. You can say that Walt Disney made a impact in my life Walt Disney helped me and my grandfather have a special bond together like before I thanked Walt Disney one hundred percent.

I feel like that Walt Disney is my very best friend somebody I could turn to during my hard times somebody that I feel relaxed turning for advice for. Like Walt Disney helped me make a special bond between me and my grandfather and I treasure every moment when I spend time with my grandfather.

Like before Disney has been a very good friend of mine I thanked him a lot growing up to teach me the deferent's between right from wrong. Even after all these years I still enjoy watching Disney films because it's still part of who I am and the special bond I had with me and my grandfather.

In my opinion here's a person went though all that trouble to make cartoons to entertain millions of people around the world and I'm very proud to be one of those millions people around the world. My opinion without images the human soul would be empty I believe in that one hundred percent.

Also I'm proud to have Walt Disney in my life as my every dearest friend to help me to have the bond between me and my grandfather. That's what Disney is all about magic going to the movies having the bond between love ones and friends enjoying life and doing the right thing all the time that's all that matters.

Everybody has their reasons why they like Disney for so many years cause Disney has that few of that magic that people want to go to the movies and have that special bond between love ones and friend. Also Disney has the special lesson that will teach the younger generations to do the right thing all the time to go out and spend a hour and play a day there's hardly that many role model that can't do that now and days.

Chapter Two

Animation has their ways on making anybody laugh bring joy to children's all over the world they bring some happiness into their life's. Not only children they bring happiness into their life's they also bring happiness to adults cause you are never to old to watch the things you love or to old to do the things you like I believe in that.

During the early years of animation everything was in black and white but still all of the animation are still good it doesn't matter if it's in black and white or color at long as the magic is there in Disney. Thru out more then eight decades the very first cartoon that appeared on the big screen then everything started to change forever something that no one will ever imagine in there life.

Walt Disney always told me growing up to set free on your imagination because I believe without imagination the human soul will be empty I believe in that completely. Cause imagination is a big part of our lives you have to learn to express it everywhere just like Walt Disney did every day at his work place and Walt Disney express it all over the world and became part of our life's for everybody.

The very first animation that came to the big screen is "Steamboat Willie" the reason why that is a very special cartoon cause it's the very first one that ever came out as cartoon. Also it's the very first to ever use sounds cause before Steamboat Willie everything wasn't used by sound that's why it's so special for everybody that's a big Disney fan.

At first Steamboat Willie staring Mickey Mouse was in black and white but nobody cared it's still a good cartoon and everybody loved it no matter what even I. Around 1932 "Flowers and Trees" was the very first cartoon that ever been used for color and ever blown out of there mind even today. Even though and I'm only twenty six years old I'm still impressed cause they worked every hard on those colors to put into that colored cartoon cause they put the effort into it a lot.

Mickey Mouse is the biggest star in the Walt Disney Studio cause he's the biggest break that Walt Disney has ever had. It's like a friendship between Walt Disney and Mickey Mouse have just like the friendship between me and Walt Disney and my grandfather which I love so much and our friendship grown since I was a little boy.

Back in those days colors were very exceptive but now in days colors are not so exceptive and back in those days when they didn't have the colors they put it in so the children of today can enjoy watching it. Some of the Disney movies today show some of the classic cartoons before the movie starts to show those young generations how cartoons were back in those days and the effort they put into them.

Snow White and the Seven Dwarfs is the first live action animation movie that's ever been made back in 1938 and be on the big screen which I love watching over and over again. The reason why Snow White is so special is because it has the magic touch that goes into any animation movie that bring that special bond between people.

Snow White and the Seven Dwarfs is such a popular movie it has gone up the big screen more than four times thru out the twentieth centaury. It might even go up again in the twenty first centaury on the big screen that's how popular that Snow White and the Seven Dwarfs is.

It took them four years to make Snow White and the Seven Dwarfs because it's such a big thing to the Walt Disney Studio. I'm very proud of the Walt Disney Studio for working so hard on such a good picture like Snow White and the Seven Dwarfs. All of the Dwarfs have their own different characters that speak for themselves to make the story so great after so many years.

Mostly The Jungle Book has been very special. It's been looked out after because it was Walt Disney's last work before Walt Disney passed on. The Disney version is much better because back in the late 1960's they really put the effort into it with all of the different characters could really speak for themselves thru out these many years. If Walt Disney is still around he well be very proud on how much of a impact that movie made thru out these many years and he might be speechless.

Thru out many years the Walt Disney Studio made hundreds of hits in the big screen and everybody in the Disney Studio are very proud of there work. Pushing technically to make everybody to believe reach for a star do the right thing all the time and get out a hour and have fun in life. That's what Walt Disney teach me growing up and the bond me and my grandfather had for so many years which I'm very proud that my grandfather introduce me to Disney at a young age.

Toy Story came from Pixar Animation Studio it's part of Walt Disney Studio broken new technology on animation forever. It's all about what will happen if no one is around when toys are around in their own little world. The movie tells you that you always have a friend it doesn't matter what you are from the outside but who you are from the inside that's all it really matter judge only from the inside not from the outside.

Since 1938 when Snow White and the Seven Dwarfs came out to the big screen the Academy Awards have accepted animation as part of their own. Walt Disney is the every first to ever accept award for best animation and to Disney fans including myself are very proud of that which The Walt Disney Studio have won more awards then any other studio and still go today.

Later on life other awards are born like the Golden Globes and the Emmys which Walt Disney has won most of the awards like crazy. In my book Walt Disney is a genius he is a very crateful person who knows what he was S doing thru out his years. One thing about the Walt Disney Studio is a great story and take it onto a new twist what makes the Walt Disney Studio so great thru out so many years.

Chapter Three

———————— ◆ ————————

There is so many different characters that have been created at the Walt Disney Studio it's so hard to choose which one is your favorite since they made so many in the studio. One thing about the Walt Disney Studio is a good story they enjoy having and change it around to make the characters different and unique in their own way.

Thru out the decades in Disney animation there is full of magic but mostly there's been animals that the Walt Disney Studio have been using and all of those animals play there own unique characters. In my opinion people are surprised to see animals playing their own unique characters since The Walt Disney studio used their first animal like Mickey Mouse.

Walt Disney Studio has one animal to thank for and that's Mickey Mouse since he is a mouse and it all started by one mouse on Steamboat Willie back in 1928. Mickey Mouse and Walt Disney have a every good partnership and friendship together thru out their career.

All of those characters have their own unique way of making their marks in the Disney Studio cause they leave their own unique ways. My all time favorite Disney character is Pluto because he doesn't talk but make body language in his own unique way.

People best know American favorite icon Mickey Mouse is The Band Concert because that's when Mickey give his finest role ever. Personally that's how I remembered Mickey

Mouse also but Mickey Mouse first started in Steamboat Willie and kicked off something that no one was expecting.

All of the Disney characters have their own unique way on making their own marks in everybody's life. It really doesn't matter what characters it is everybody has a favorite character in the Disney family as long as it has a special meaning to there favorite character. Like how Pluto is my all time favorite character one of the first major animation dog star.

Everybody in life that enjoys watching Disney films have their own way remembering Disney and they are hooked for life. It could be any Disney film it doesn't matter if it's live animation movie or live action movie as long as they remember Walt Disney putting the magic into it. My personal favorite movie is The Jungle Book because that was Walt Disney's last work before he passed on putting that last bit of magic into it.

Question is how they touch everybody in life? All of the Disney films have a way that touch everybody's life's in their own way. My way is The Jungle Book the way that Walt Disney put the magic into cause I see all the deferent's version they made into that classic story. One thing about the Disney Studios is they always putting a new twist into so they can make it more fun and music into it.

The Walt Disney Studio always have that magic into lathery classic that's how everybody remembered and how they touch everybody's life. So far I'm very proud that Walt Disney has touched me with the bond between me and my grandfather we had thru out so many years. Like before after all these years I still enjoy watching Disney films even animations.

Walt Disney has his own way to touch everybody in life even me growing up and very proud that he did with me teaching me the deferent's between right from wrong and the bond between me and my grandfather. I'm sure that Disney has touched everybody else life's also bringing them the same bond between their own family and friends.

Best way to remember them in their own unique way it doesn't matter if it's a live action film or even live action animations movie everybody has a way to remember them. I personally will best remember is Pluto cause he never talks or anything but use body languages and the way he move his face.

Personally I collected all of the Disney stuff so I always remembered my favorite characters so I will never forget no matter what. Some times I always enjoying see the villains of most Disney films and all of the time the villains always lose but all of the villains are unique in their own way something that the Walt Disney Studio will never let you see.

I know for sure that Monopoly has a collectors edition of Disney villains to see what they know about their villains which in my option is a good thing because every good story needs a villain even in the Walt Disney Studio. Without the villains the story wont have any meaning so I always did like the villains better even if they do lose.

A lot of people that enjoys watching the villains are always enjoys watching the Disney villains better cause Disney puts the real magic into those villains. The classic villains always had that magic during the golden ages of animations and that's how most be best remember.

Thru out the years Peter Pan was usually played by a girl but Walt Disney broke that rule and let a boy play that role. That's how most people remember the Disney version and everybody enjoys the Disney version that Walt Disney created thru out the years even with the sequel it was still played by a boy.

All of these characters have their own unique way that leaves their own marks and everybody will remember them for now and future generation. I speak for every Disney characters out there they have their own way to touch us on our own way just like when Pinocchio touched me with the bond between me and my grandfather.

Even if you are a baby you will enjoy watching Disney Channel and watching Disney films with somebody you love thru out the years. I should know I went thru the same thing when I was a little baby with my grandfather watching Disney films. The magic thru out the years with Disney will never change as long as there's imagination in the world and people will believe.

Chapter Four

───────── ◈ ─────────

Like all major studios all of them made so many great live action movies and the Walt Disney Studios is one of them. There were so many good live action movies that the Walt Disney Studio made it is so hard to choose in my opinion all of the Disney films have there own kind of way of putting magic inside of the movies.

My opinion the real magic is the people behind the camera that made the movies extra special thru out these many years. I give them all credit for working the extra mile to make all these movies very special to millions of children and adults like me growing up and my grandfather.

The first live action film that Walt Disney made was Treasure Island for live imagination and lot of action to watch over and over again. Also it's the very first to use pirates so kids could enjoy watching live action pirates getting into mischief and the rest is history. Since Treasure Island the Walt Disney Studio made more live action films all thanks to Treasure Island.

My personal favorite live action Walt Disney movie is Old Yeller cause it's about a bond between a boy and his dog just like the bond between me and my grandfather when I was young. These classic Disney movies all have a special meaning to them to bring family closer just like me and my grandfather.

Like many Disney films it doesn't matter if it's live action films or animation most of them have villains and everybody needs a good villain that everybody loves to hate. Some of the Disney films don't have villains but true Disney fans don't care like myself I really don't care if there is a villain or not in Disney films cause all of them are pretty wonderful to watch.

My all time favorite villain is well it's hard to choose cause all of them are pretty good it makes no deferent's who the villain is all of them are unique in their special way. So I like all of the villains that the Walt Disney Studio has made thru out the years so I have a lot of respect for all of the animators that made so many great villains of all the great movies they made.

Makes no deferent's back then and now on all of the movies they made all of them are pretty good but now days every movie is made pretty easy by computers. Computers have changed everything for more than twenty years they bring visual effects to life to capture our imagination like crazy even on animation.

Animation is first is drawn on paper and pencil and then they get put into computers so they could do the really hard stuff something that the Disney Studio couldn't do back during the early years of animation. Back in the olden days without computers you felt alive with the animation just like the kids of today are alive on the animation done by computers.

Now a days the computers broke right in technically on Pixar Toy Story the very first computer animated ever and did it to blow everybody out of there minds. It's like nothing that anybody has ever seen in their whole life before. Toy Story is about what every happens when your toys are all alone it's something that I never dream of seeing before the movie is wonderful so much imagination is in it.

Walt Disney Studio loves pushing technically all the time and Toy Story was the first computer animation of one of them thru out the years back then and now. Also the Walt Disney Studio is the first to bring animatronics to the world in Disneyland and thru out the world. Back in the 1950's animatronics was a band new world when Disneyland was born.

Back then there was barrel any colors inside the pictures even the cartoon but now a days there's color for everything on television and movies all thanks to Walt Disney. Walt Disney was the first to bring color into pictures it really didn't matter if it was cartoon or not.

The first color was back in 1932 on "Flowers and Trees" but back in those days they were very expensive but now a days their not expensive. When "Flowers and Trees" came out in theaters everybody was blown out of their mind seeing colors for the first time it's like something that they never seen before in the big screen.

Back in the early twentieth century television wasn't invented yet so people went to see the news and the movie in the theaters but in the middle of the 1940's all the way to early 1950's television was invented. Television was invented people are starting to stay home and relax to watch in the convert of their home and Walt Disney is one of those people that took advantage of television.

Walt Disney started the Mickey Mouse Club when television was born in those days and had one popular star and that was Annette. They made two different version of Mickey Mouse Club both was good during the mid 1950 and early 1990's. Also they made Wonderful World of Disney showing all these different worlds that Disney created.

Now at these days everything is done by sequels now because some people want to know what happen like what happened after wards. My all time favorite all time sequels is Jungle Book 2 because the Jungle Book has been special look out after since it was Walt Disney last work. It tells me what happened after wards when the boy goes into the village does he come back to the jungle or not.

There's a few more classics they made sequels after words Peter Pan, Cinderella are a few that they made sequels their still good no matter what. Both of those sequels tells what happen after wards after happily every after so far everybody has a favorite sequel like me and true Disney fans out there in the world.

Music is one of the big part of Disney without music in animations or live action movies without any music's you wont get into the movie that much. Thru out the ages of the Walt Disney Studio music is really part of who Walt Disney is. Even on the first computer animation Pixar Toy Story they use music to show part of the animation it's like part of the animation and movies almost.

My all time favorite Disney music is Pixar Cars Real Gone because it has that special magic into it cause I use to work at hobbies shop once when I was young sailing toy cars to little kids. I like cars a lot and Disney Pixar Cars and the song Real Gone brings back a lot of good members working in the hobbies shop.

Everybody has a favorite Disney sequel or favorite Disney film or favorite television show from Disney like me if you are a Disney fan I proud to grow up with Disney he's a big part of who I am. It's the bond I had with me and my grandfather growing up I thanked Walt Disney a lot for the bond I had with somebody like my grandfather.

Walt Disney isn't afraid pushing technically isn't afraid pushing the enveloped on new things like the first to bring color to animation or the first computer animated like Pixar Toy Story also the first to bring sounds to a major cartoon. So far Walt Disney told me don't be afraid on who you want to be or what you want to do in life never every be afraid of anything.

Chapter Five

Disneyland so far it's been named after Walt Disney himself its the most happiest place on earth I have been there so many times I lost count cause it's my favorite place on earth I go as much as I can every year. Six Flags Magic Mountain doesn't come close to all what Disneyland has cause Disneyland has that magic touch with family and children who can go together and have fun at the same time.

Mickey Mouse also same goes with all of the other Disney stars made more guess appearances in theme park then any other theme park put together that's one of the reason why Disneyland is special. The other reason why Disneyland is special is people dress up there favorite characters as much as they want in one theme park without anybody caring what anybody thinks about them.

I feel like that Disneyland is a free place to act freely to be a child and act like adult at the same time without anybody knowing. Best thing about Disneyland is it's everywhere in the world there's two in America one in Europe and two in Asia so everybody could go to the happiest place on earth without any trouble so everybody could enjoy the happiness in one theme park.

It all started by one mouse name Mickey Mouse everybody should say thank you to Mickey Mouse without Mickey Mouse Disneyland would never happen or Walt Disney helping on setting free with your imaginations. When Walt Disney created Mickey Mouse and Disneyland he was a genius he was way ahead of his time and still is on his passing today and everything is passed down.

My opinion is that the hardest character to take a picture with is Mickey Mouse because Mickey is the one who started all this when Walt Disney hit the spot with Mickey Mouse. Personally my favorite characters is Pluto cause I'm a dog lover since I was a little boy.

Sunday July 17 1955 that's when Disneyland was first born around the summer time that's when children are out of school so it could be easy to come to Disneyland without any trouble. The first day that the park was open everything went crazy foods went out and one of the rides caught on fire but nothing seriously.

Beside the fact that everything went bad everybody in the park had a good time without any trouble most of the rides are fun to go on. It was a historic day for Walt Disney and for everybody that works for Walt Disney Studio something that everybody will never forget no matter what in the future.

Once every ten years Disneyland celebrates it's birthday it's such a big deal because Disneyland is a good theme park for children and adults to have fun. When it hit the fiftieth anniversary it was a big deal because it's not everyday you turn the fiftieth anniversary I should know I was there having the time of my life. I even saw Mickey Mouse putting the fiftieth anniversary flag on the Matter horn it's a very big deal for the big Disney fans like myself.

The rides are great to ride on for children and adults it doesn't matter how old you are as long as you have fun on your favorite rides that's all that matters. Disneyland always brings new rides every year or bring back old rides so that the new generations will enjoy it for now and forever.

My favorite ride well. . . .it's hard to tell I like all of the rides it makes no deferent's all of the are fun to ride on. One ride I'm not surprise that they made a movie out of and that's Pirates of the Caribbean with a few sequels on it the ride and the movie are pretty good and I'm proud to go on that ride anytime.

Also some of the rides also are Hunted Mansion, Indianan Jones and Star Wars popular movies that are rides in Disneyland. I enjoyed riding them all the time without any trouble Walt Disney must be proud of himself for what he's done on every ride he made pushing for new rides every year.

Some of the rides have been there since the theme park first opened it's doors but nobody cares at long as the rides are fun the reason why its been there cause nobody can get enough of it. Even better there's always a parade everyday to see everyone's favorite characters to take pictures all that stuff even there is some classic cars from 1929 to 1951.

Walt Disney always comes to his magic kingdom Disneyland cause he's proud of what he has done what I believe that Walt Disney always told me "Set Free With Your Imagination" That's what I have been doing since I was little boy and I'm a writer to make on impact to other young children just like Walt Disney did to me and my grandfather.

To tell you the truth I'm not surprise to see movies and television stars going to Disneyland to have fun also like normal people. First star that came to Disneyland did the news report on Disneyland on the first day later become Present of the United States around the 1980's and that's Ronald Regan.

Since then lots of stars came to Disneyland to enjoy life and get onto the rides just like everybody else and take pictures with their favorite Disney characters. I believe that everybody should go to Disneyland because it is the happiest place on earth if you are a true Disney fan it doesn't matter where you come from or who you are.

Best thing about Disneyland is you can buy anything you want I mean anything for the piece of memory of the happiest place on earth. Me I love to collect all Disney collectibles like mugs, snow–globes, pins, and toys stuff like that because you can always have something to remember about Disney always.

So far Disneyland has everything you need you name it they got it like a normal theme park so far you can't go anywhere without seeing collectibles to remember your visit. I know in my heart that Walt Disney wouldn't want you leave Disneyland without having a piece of the theme park no matter who you are or where you came from.

My favorite snow–globe is Mickey Mouse in the Steamboat Willie with some of the Disney characters around him celebrating his 75 years old. To me that's a big deal because everybody should celebrate there birthday no matter how big or small it is you should celebrate your birthday.

I'm sure that all of the other snow–globes are wonderful also makes no deferent's what so every. The people who created these Disney snow–globes are pretty good they always find creative ways of find new ways to catch peoples eyes. Also the mugs my favorite mugs are One Hundred One Dalmatian mugs because I'm a big dog lover since I was a little boy.

There's all kinds of ways to collect Disney stuff to remember you trip to Disneyland so you will never forget of your happy memories of Disneyland with friends or family. You see Disneyland has that special thing being part of the magic no matter who you are as long as you are a fan of Walt Disney and like going to Disneyland all the time you just got to believe in yourself.

There is so much to do in Disneyland where you can enjoy yourself and try to do everything at once and have fun that's all that matters. I always did enjoy going to Disneyland cause it's part of who I am and I'm very proud of it. Every time I go to Disneyland I feel like a kid in a candy store there's some magic between me and going to Disneyland every time.

Chapter Six

Walt Disney is a very special person who helped me to have the bond between me and my grandfather and that's the same thing he done with everybody else all over the world. Disney has that special magic that everybody enjoys feeling special inside of them like feeling good for themselves. Understanding what the people want is a every hard thing to do but Walt Disney understands what people want on animations and live action films.

Thru out the twentieth century the Walt Disney Studios done captured our imagination in a way that no one has every Walt Disney made an impact in my life to become who I wanted to be. To me Walt Disney is a very nice and caring person who cares about other's before he cares about himself cause he showed so much imagination to the world.

I always believe if you got so much imagination you should express it to the world that's the message that Walt Disney tells me. Cause Walt Disney has so much imagination and he express it to the world in all of his animation movies and live action movies. To me Walt Disney is a very creative person who knows how to tell story's like other has every did.

Mickey Mouse and Walt Disney have a good friendship just like me and my grandfather did so many years it's the bond between them which they had just like me and my grandfather had. Both me and my grandfather always did enjoy watching Disney films and going to Disneyland a lot and we got Walt Disney to thank for.

One thing about Walt Disney that he always pushing technically in his early career like he's the first to bring the first live action animation movie like Snow White and the Seven Dwarfs. I feel like I got to know Walt Disney for so many years he got a lot of imaginations inside of him just like me growing up.

If Walt Disney is still around he well be surprised to see Pixar Toy Story the first computer animation he will know that his way of pushing technical still works today. Also if Walt Disney sees all the new stuff that's been invented he'll push it to the next step. That's what Walt Disney always told me never to be afraid to try new things taking it to the next step on who you what to be and doing the things you like.

Walt Disney idea's are genius he always finds a way of entertaining people in a whole new way pushing technically into movies and his magic kingdom Disneyland. Some times it takes years to get a good ride at Disneyland because they want to make it right so people well be speechless on the rides.

Idea's are usually good for the human soul because they show the creative ways for the human soul so show yourself on how creative you can get inside your mind. Walt Disney always pushed his ideas and mind into so many stuff but he didn't give up no matter what. That's a good example to anybody to never give up on your dream pushing yourself into great things.

Disneyland is a good example if Walt Disney didn't push his imaginations and ideas Disneyland well never be born and millions of people wonted have fun at the most happiest place on earth. If Walt Disney went all that trouble just to make the most happiest place on earth that can so you what you can do it at long as you put your mind into it.

Walt Disney ideas are legendary something that no one will ever do cause Walt Disney is a geneses inside his mind. Push the story lines into a whole new meaning giving children something to believe in for themselves which I'm every proud what Walt Disney did for me having that bond between me and my grandfather.

The main question I always wanted to know growing up is Where does Walt Disney get all these great ideas? I always enjoy watching Disney films but where does he get all these great ideas on making all of these movies every magical to millions of children's around the world. Only place that's where the magic is inside of Walt Disney that's the only answers that I know inside of my mind.

Where ever that answer is on where Walt Disney gets his idea is everywhere to me Walt Disney is a every good story teller and proud of it and I'm every lucky that I'm part of that magic watching Disney films. I believe everybody should have that magic inside there life's just like Walt Disney has plan inside his films I know that for a fact cause he bring some magic inside my life just like everybody else's life.

In Walt Disney studio they have so many ideas to capture the magic inside all of us to show you to set free your imagination be yourself and do the right thing all the time. I believe in that all the time thanks to Walt Disney and my grandfather to introduce me to Walt Disney and so much in life.

Walt Disney left one good legacy to everybody he always enjoys pushing technically creating new things in life and make a popular theme park named after him. Leaving a good legacy tells me a lot of a person on what they leave behind and that's what Walt Disney did he left something to the good people all over the world something to believe in themselves.

Legacy of Walt Disney is always wish upon a star makes no deferent's how big or small it is as long as you believe in yourself. Also never care what other people think about you as long as what you think of yourself that's all that really matters and do the right thing. To me that's what Walt Disney tells me growing up and I thank Walt Disney about that all the time growing up watching his films.

I'm very proud on what Walt Disney's legacy and it's still passed down from generation to generation after his passing. Even when Walt Disney passed on the Walt Disney Studio still stands and doing animation and also blockbuster films Walt Disney did so much for us and me I owe a thank you to Walt Disney so much.

Leaving a legacy to somebody is very important just like what Walt Disney did to everybody all over the world Walt Disney left so much magic and that's way the legacy he did to me he left some magic inside of me. Walt Disney also left a legacy to my grandfather the first time that my grandfather went to Disneyland my grandfather was every impressed and glad to come Disneyland being part of some great.

Walt Disney had so many loyal fans thru out so many years since Mickey Mouse came out in Steam Willie back in 1928 everybody that enjoys watching Mickey knows that they are hooked. Also when everybody saw Snow White and the Seven Dwarfs the very first live action animation movie everybody was really hooked to Disney for good.

I have been a loyal fan to Disney since I was just a young child since the very first movie I saw with my grandfather seeing Pinocchio. The second time we saw Pinocchio me and my grandfather know right away that we were hooked for life loyal to Walt Disney after all these years. Being loyal to Walt Disney after all these years were the best time of my life watching so many great movies and television shows.

Right now a lot of loyal Walt Disney fans collectors Disney because no one can have enough of Walt Disney I should know I collected a lot of Walt Disney collectibles. Walt Disney touch us a lot and I'm loyal to Walt Disney's work from his early starts from Mickey Mouse on Steamboat Willie till forever.

Chapter Seven

Headlines and legends thru out history there's always headlines and legends of famous people and one of those people I grow up knowing is Walt Disney. Walt Disney has more headlines then any other studio founders have ever made before and Walt Disney is very proud of himself to be on the public eye so many times. No surprise that Walt Disney become a legend cause of all the hard work Walt Disney made with his imagination and share it all over the world.

The reason why Walt Disney made more appearance as a studio's founder then any other because he's the first to bring animation to the world better then any other has bring animation to the world. Walt Disney breaks and brings new technical things to the world that's why he became a legend in his own way to the world.

Another reason why Walt Disney become so much in the headlines because of the awards that Walt Disney has won so many times because he understands what the people want and how to animate pretty well like no other does. That's why Walt Disney became headline and legend cause he earn that way to the top like no other studio founder has ever done.

Even after all these years Walt Disney still became a headline but he still remains a legend after all the landmarks that Walt Disney made thru out the years by the breakthrough.

Since Walt Disney has won more Academy Awards then any other studio that's why Walt Disney made Headlines and Legend.

I know in my heart that Walt Disney will never let himself go to his head when he become a headline and legend. Walt Disney is a very warm caring person who cares about others before he cares about himself and that's a fact. If a person went to all that trouble just to make some unique characters to entertain for more then millions of people to me that's quit a person and that's Walt Disney.

Best thing about Walt Disney is that he's a very gentle man a down to earth caring wonderful person never let who his fame cloud his better judgment. The one's that know Walt Disney better could tell you that cause Walt Disney is a very warm person if you ever meet him you feel like you are on top of the world.

I should be on top of the world if I ever meet Walt Disney I will be on top of the world cause I enjoy his work on animation movies and live action movies. Everybody that's a big Walt Disney fan like myself will tell you that Walt Disney is a every creative person who really understands what people want in animations.

When Walt Disney passed on everybody in the department looked out after the company so that the magic would stay magic cause like Walt Disney cares about his fans just like everybody in head of the department. I'm very proud of the head of the department to look out after Walt Disney Studios. Taking care of something like a studio is a lot of responsible work I give them a lot of credit.

Just like the Jungle Book that was Walt Disney's last work before he passed on has been specially looked out after. When the sequel came from the Jungle Book it's been really been careful on the continualness on something special like this that's where the magic is and still on after all these years.

I know in my heart that Walt Disney never care of being famous all he ever cares about is the fans giving them good entertment on animation like Mickey Mouse on Steamboat Willie. Walt Disney is the very first person that ever used sound back in 1928 if a person went to all that trouble just to show some entertainment who doesn't care of being famous to me is a very good and truthful person.

Walt Disney to me is a person who really enjoys pushing technically just like me pushing myself to write good stories for children. So you can say that Walt Disney and me got something in common we both like pushing ourselves into new things and also care about other's before we care about ourselves.

Fame is not only everything in life I'm sure that Walt Disney cares about life so he could enjoy it like the making of Old Yeller. In that area where they made Old Yeller Walt Disney went to that area just to relax and concentrate of all his work and not let fame bug him in his good judgment Walt Disney enjoyed life just like everybody else.

Royalties are not important in life as long as what you like that's all it matters at long as you like what you are doing. Walt Disney spent his whole life entertaining young children like me with the special bond between me and my grandfather that's all it matter the bond between your friends and love ones that's all it matters and I'm sure that Walt Disney didn't care about the money.

Because Walt Disney teach me a lot of stuff growing up the deferent's between right from wrong and bring a lot of laughter inside my life and bring me the bond between me and my grandfather. I know in my heart that Walt Disney never care about the royalties as long as he brought a lot of joy to peoples life's that's all that mattered and that's what Walt Disney did.

During the early years at the Walt Disney Studio Walt and Mickey had a every special partnership a very strong working relationship. Something that no one will ever break they have a special bond together just like all bonds all over the world. A bond and a partnership will never be broken no matter what because there's some magic between the partnership between Mickey Mouse and Walt Disney.

Without Mickey Mouse and Walt Disney working together they would never built Disneyland or the Walt Disney Studio or any other Disney characters. Thru out the ages in the Walt Disney Studio they break technically Steamboat Willie is the first to bring sounds thanks to Walt Disney. Thanks to Mickey Mouse Walt Disney hit a bullseye to Mickey since then a good partnership is born and breaking technically for now and forever.

Thru out the ages at the Walt Disney Studio there's been all kinds of thing that captured our imagination but mostly there's been animals. You don't see that there are animals because you see them as people to bring the magic into the movies and that's what Walt Disney has been doing.

Walt Disney and the studio did a lot of magic thru these many years it doesn't matter if it's animals or not or pushing technically all that matter's is that the magic is there and the bond between love ones and friends. It doesn't matter if Walt Disney won a lot of awards or fame or royalties he brought the magic into the movies with something we never seen before that's what matters.

I'm very proud of what Walt Disney did with me he showed me the bond between me and my grandfather something that no one will ever take away that's what Walt Disney did for me. I know for sure that the future of the Walt Disney Studio will do that same thing on future generations and I'm proud on what they done and are still doing.

I like everything about Walt Disney I collected Disney collectibles to remind me about how important having fun is and the bond between me and my grandfather and the joyfulness on how important life is. For sure I know this for a fact that everybody in the Walt Disney Studio are happy on what they are doing bringing a lot of magic into young generations of children bringing them laughter action and advetnure in their young life's.

Chapter Eight

◈

One thing that the Walt Disney Studio always enjoys is a good story cause without a good story the Walt Disney Studio wouldn't be alive today. It's like open imagination without any imagination the story wouldn't have any meaning at all. Story's always have a special meaning to anybody cause it's maybe their favorite they could enjoy watching it over and over again.

During the early years of Walt Disney animations were a lot different till today cause everything is done by computers to be a lot easier. If you seen the deferent's back in those days and today's you see the deferent's alright without any trouble. Today's animations are done by drawing by paper and pencil then they could put it in the computer to make it a lot easier.

The most treasured work of Walt Disney is the Jungle Book because it's the last work of Walt Disney before he passed on. It has that hard work and magic into it before computers are born it had that paper and pencil magic into it. That's why most people remembered the Walt Disney classic animations better then any other of today's animations.

Story's is a big part of any major movie studio even for the Walt Disney Studio each of the other studio puts their magic into it but at the Walt Disney Studio they take magic very seriously with story's. Every story's needs a good villain because without any villains the story wont make any sense. You can say that villains are the big part of the story cause I always did enjoy seeing the villains better then the heroes.

Reason why I like watching the villains better because they come all different shapes and sizes to me without the villains there aren't any story's. Villains are the main reason why there are story's and Walt Disney captured our imagination on all of the villains in his story's to share to the world.

That's why I like that Walt Disney story's cause he captured our imaginations on every story's he makes thru out his career and tell now. To me Walt Disney is a every gifted person who knows how to tell story's for millions of children and adults all over the world and Walt Disney express it everyday.

Walt Disney version on making good animation is always putting that magic into it but the way Walt Disney makes the version on any animation is usually fantastic putting the magic into it. The reason why the Disney films have that magic into it is that they really put that effort into the animation.

What I mean on the effort into The Lion King it took them five years to make that film cause they took their time to make it very special to millions of children around the world like myself. The Lion King is kind of like Hamlet one of William Shakespeare's great novel and turn it around used animals and made a blockbuster animation film.

Peter Pan is another version that Walt Disney made into special usually Peter Pan is played by a girl but Walt Disney broke that rule made Peter Pan into a boy. Also the dog nana come to Never Land but nana didn't come to Never Land but either way the Walt Disney version is wonderful.

Walt Disney version in a literary classic always have that magic inside of it no matter how Walt Disney changes it always has that special magic into it and that's why everybody remembered the Walt Disney version better. That's why the Disney films always has the special magic into them cause Walt Disney puts that special magic into it so no one forgets it.

I got to admit thru out the ages of Walt Disney Studio there's always been animals putting the magic into Walt Disney Studio cause without the animals in the Walt Disney Studio there well be no studio like Walt Disney. Just like Mickey Mouse on the 1928 Steamboat Willie it all started by one mouse starting the magic into it and it well never end.

Thru out so many years at the Walt Disney Studio there's always been magic capturing our imaginations in so many ways. One of those magic's is the way Walt Disney uses timeless story's and giving them a new twist giving them some magic inside of them and giving them a different version.

Without magic of a Walt Disney movies the story well never have meaning into it. Just like Disneyland Walt Disney put a lot of magic into it and people feel the magic right inside of you even all of the Disney films. Magic is the job in Walt Disney Studio it's a big part of who they are even Walt Disney himself.

Chapter Nine

————————— ◆ —————————

Future of Walt Disney Studio is always there in the passed and the future pushing technically bring new ways to entertained millions of children's and adults at longs as they believe. It all started by one mouse name of Mickey Mouse on Steamboat Willie in 1928 the every first cartoon that every use sounds. Since then Walt Disney hit a bull's– eyes pushing technically into major motion pictures and people well never forget at long as you are a big Disney fan.

Second biggest thing that Walt Disney think about in the future is putting colors into animations and that's 1932 Flowers and Trees the every first to use color and that paid the ways of other's to use color. That's what the future of the Walt Disney is all about pushing technically and making people believe in themselves and doing the right thing that's the message what Walt Disney is always showing before and after his passing.

Also the future of animations is the every first animated movie back in 1938 was Snow White and the Seven Dwarfs. Bring that kind of technically make people believe that anything is possible in life at long as you believe in yourself just like Walt Disney did on making the every first animated film every.

Right now the newest technically is computer animations like Walt Disney Pixar's Toy Story the every first computer animated every that blown peoples imaginations like no other. Thanks to the hard work and effort of the Pixar Animation Studio bring something like these to everybody's these is something that no one every seen before.

Future of Walt Disney in the twenty first century is here now on compacted D.V.D's which all of major classic and newest movies that came from Disney could come to D.V.D's to show how they make the film. It doesn't matter if it's animations or live action movies at long as you enjoy watching your favorite movies or animations films.

There's so many changes coming to Walt Disney Studio you just have to come and see if yourself I can't reveal all of Walt Disney Studio or at Disneyland you just have to waited and see. In the future there well be so many magic well come to the younger generations to enjoy have the privilege of Walt Disney inside there life's.

Some of the rides do become movies in Disneyland cause the rides remand so popular and remand in one theme for so many years. There's a few of those rides in Disneyland that came to the big screen but at the same time remand truthful to the ride of the theme park. One of those rides become a couple of sequels cause the first movie become a blockbuster.

A popular ride become a smash hit to the blockbusters is Pirates of the Caribbean. Pirates of the Caribbean has been at Disneyland since 1968 and has been there every since. I should I know I rode that ride so many time I know the history about that ride it's the last idea from Walt Disney before he passed on back in the late 1960's.

The first Pirate of the Caribbean movie came out it did more then it accepted that's why they made two sequel and those two did pretty well. I'm every proud of the director and everybody else of Pirate of the Caribbean movies they did wonderful job on making that movie they stayed loyal to the ride to make these movie.

On Pirate of the Caribbean they put a lot of good sword fighting into it which may I add is every good because on the ride they have sword fighting. In my opinion they did a every good job and the sequel are even more good then the first. Without the sword fighting in the movie it wonted make senesces so they did a good job on all three films.

Haunted Madison is the most popular ride it's been there since Disneyland was open and has been there every since. That's one of my favorite rides I go there as much as I can every time I go to Disneyland usually that's the first ride I would like to go on first. When they made the movie I'm glad that they stayed loyal to the ride because if you stay loyal to the ride the movie well be a blockbuster hit one hundred percent.

The movie of the Haunted Madison is fantastic it got everything in it without any trouble the director put a lot of imaginations into it to make these movie every successful and special. Putting somebody like comedian Eddie Murphy into Hunted Madison is wonderful something that no one well every think of.

Movies that become rides are a work of geniuses because there's some movies are so popular that they have to make a ride but don't know how. With a little imaginations they have something that more then enough on a ride that's going to last for a every long time. There's two popular rides that has been successful for so many years which I'm hoping that they well never go away.

First movie that come as a ride is Star Wars back in 1977 all three films did more then enough on the blockbusters. So no surprise that they made a ride inside Disneyland you feel like your inside space riding along having a hole lot of fun. They made really look alike space ship so you can feel like you are going inside space something you can't replace.

When you go inside near the ride you could see really druids like R2–D2 and other's you remember from all three movies. One thing about the rides and the movie they have to stay loyal from the movie when they are making the ride because if you don't the ride wonted be popular and no one well wasted there time on the ride. The second movie that came to a popular is Indiana Jones since they made four popular films out of it I don't know if they making a five movie but I hope that make another Indiana Jones. Since all three originally films are fantastic I'm not a less surprise that they made a Indiana Jones ride in Disneyland.

Best thing about these Indiana Jones ride is you seat inside of a car and go crazy on a really good ride. The ride have some of the movie inside of it enough to go crazy you never know what to expected if it's your first time. When you get use to it you well still enjoy it because if you are a big Indiana Jones fan like myself you well never get board out of it.

Those are the two movies that they made into rides in the most happiest ride on earth so far no one well every get enough out of it. If you enjoy watching the movies and never get board out of it then you well never get board to go inside the ride no matter what. Also if you enjoy the other rides in Disneyland go for it you are never to old to do the things you like and don't care what other people think about you all it matters what you think about yourself.

Changes it always happens in all major studio because change happens you can't do anything about it. Evangel there going to make the studio much bigger cause you need the room to make more movies or something. At the Disneyland and any other theme park they have make changes because without changes cause how long you can keep up the same thing.

Some things well stay the same like the magic of Walt Disney and Disneyland because everybody needs a little magic inside there life's. Something change in life and something don't change in life I got to admit to that but I'm happy that some things haven't changed and that's the life of magic in the Walt Disney.

Chapter Ten

———————— ◆ ————————

December 7 1941 when Japan hit Pearl Harbor Walt Disney Studio had a hard hit Walt Disney Studio went thru a seriously times. Like a normal job everybody were going thru hard time's also but some how the Walt Disney Studio wonted give up no matter what just like everybody else. Everybody were determent to go thru the hard times to get a chance to make it thru to make the extra living.

Walt Disney took advance thru the hard times and made serial cartoon shorts about during the wars to see how everybody goes thru these hard times. At lease the young children's knows that war isn't a good thing but a idea what they go thru on basic training and hope that these war well end peacefully.

What happen during those years is that Walt Disney lost a lot of money during those times cause the European weren't showing the Disney film like he hopes. But Walt Disney isn't going to give up like most studio founders they are determent to make good films and make good animations.

Like most of the studio they lose two third of profited but all of these studio have one thing in common they are not welling to give up without making good pictures and Walt Disney is one of them. Walt Disney still had that magic thru out the war making good war cartoons and be proud to live in a free country.

Walt Disney showed everybody in the country be grateful that you live in a free country and never take advanced on your freedom. The message what Walt Disney tells me be lucky that you are living in free country that you can make your own choice without anybody telling you how to make your choices.

Second World War were so hard times thru out those four years in America but Walt Disney always has a idea to get the people inside the theater. Walt Disney created Fun and Fancies Free to build to help out the economy out beside making the war cartoon short called the Front Line to help the studio out.

During the second World War a lot of Walt Disney film were put on hold and of those films were one of my favorite was Peter Pan. Up side is that Fun and Fancies Free helped the Walt Disney Studio out giving everybody the hope they need during the war times in the early to mid 1940's and Walt Disney also.

At the end of the second World War at 1945 everything got back to normal and Walt Disney went back to making good animation movies. One of those good animation is Peter Pan it took them a every long time to make that good film all thanks to the story author Sir J.M Barrie.

I'm glad that the war ended and Walt Disney bring the magic into the movies and animations also and Europe got back to normal to see some magic. Later on everybody in Europe well have a Disneyland up in France so they could enjoy the magic of Disney no matter what ages at long as the magic is there.

Holidays are usually a big thing for most major studio but at the Walt Disney they take it every seriously because holidays is a every big deal. Walt Disney brings magic into the holidays films all the time because they take magic and holidays every seriously.

First at Disneyland they always decorate the hole theme park with Christmas decoration and have big party about it. All of the Disney characters dress up in Christmas customs the reason why they do these because everybody that loves the holidays so much and comes to Disneyland should enjoy themselves on the most happiest place on earth.

Holidays films are usually fun to make to celebrate the most happiest time of the year. My all time favorite holiday film is Mickey's Christmas Carol the reason why that all of Mickey's animated friends and star in these film it was nominated for best Academy Award for best animated short. Beside that Walt Disney made a lot of other animated shorts to for Christmas cause he believes in good well in all.

I know in my heart that Walt Disney loves the holiday season because it brings out the goodness of all people no matter who or where you come from. Even today the Walt Disney Studio still makes good holiday films for the younger generations to come to treasures when they grow up and pass it on to there children's.

Halloween is my all time favorite season because of Trick–or–Treat getting free candy and when I was a little boy I remember all the great Halloween movies that The Disney Channel shows every month of October. What's best is that the Hunted Madison always that time of the year shows the version of The Nightmare Before Christmas inside that ride.

It's every magical seeing that kind of version inside that ride without the parents saying anything it's a every good time of the year. In my opinion that's usually a good time to go to Disneyland cause your free to dress up as anything you like without anybody even saying anything cause Halloween the one time of the year you could get free candy's.

Now fun show they put on for children's now and days are also good to get the spirited of Halloween alive for anybody and I mean anybody to show the bond between every one. Christmas is also good for children's to go to Disneyland because it's time for giving and having fun also and that's what Walt Disney wants use to do.

The Walt Disney Studio survive the war year's between 1941 thru 1945 for a every long time but pulled thru and enjoys celebrating the holidays season for all ages at Disneyland. They always enjoyest putting magic cause that the number one thing that always enjoys doing spreeding magic thru out the years. It doesn't matter if you are watching the movies or even going to the theme park.

Chapter Eleven

◆

Thru out the twentieth century in the Walt Disney Studio there's always been hero's and villains without them the story wonted make senses. If you looked thru all of the Disney's films there's hero's and villains that captured our imaginations and break thru technically it well show that the hero's always wins and the villains always lose.

We started from the top with the hero's cause everybody likes the hero's because there heroic, brave and always truthful. You know that all hero's tells you to do the right thing all the time and be brave and always be truthful and never run away from your problem. Being a hero could be anybody at long as you believe in yourself and all it matters what you think of yourself.

Like take a look of Woody he's a toy cowboy he become a hero by saving Buzz Lightyear from the toy torture from next door. It doesn't matter if he's a toy or not all it matters what he think of himself and saved Buzz Lightyear and they become good friends every since from Walt Disney Pixar's Toy Story.

Also from Monsters Inc there were full of hundreds of monsters doing what they always doing scaring young children's but the end two monsters fight what they believe in. Both of them defended a human girl from a evil monsters by being kidnapped from that evil monster's plan that well show that that being a hero it doesn't matter if monsters or not being a hero is being yourself.

Also from Snow White and the Seven Dwarfs all of the seven Dwarfs came to save Snow White and the seven dwarfs didn't care what they were from the outside at long as it matter from the inside. At the end the dwarfs and the prince saved the princesses from that evil witch evil plans.

Villains I always did like the villains because the are unique that come all shape or sizes or even animals there villains. Without the villains the story wonted make senses because every good story's needs a good villain to scare or leave there mark in the Walt Disney Studio. Walt Disney Studio always put the magic into the villains because like before every good story's needs a every crazy and good villains.

Like The Jungle Book around the near ending between Mowgli and Sari Khan the villain was a human but it was a tiger. To me Sari Khan is the most scares villain I every seen in my life growing up watching Disney films because Sari Khan has that special villain scarceness that Walt Disney worked on before Walt Disney passed on.

The second all time villain I like is Captain Hook from Peter Pan because he's the every first pirate that's every been introduce to the world from Walt Disney animation. Captain Hook has that special magic being the first pirate in Walt Disney's history and to me that's something that's never going to replace.

There's always a good reason why people like the villains they have that special meaning to them just like the hero's. It doesn't matter if it's the villains or the hero's all of them have there special way making there impression to use so we can remember them for now and future generation.

I'm every proud of the Walt Disney Studio for putting so many magic into the hero's and villains because they all worked every hard with there hand and hearts. Like before every good story's needs hero's and villains because it wonted make any senesces at all. Mostly I like the villains that the Walt Disney makes and puts the magic because they have own special meaning into them.

All of them the hero's and the villains from the passed and present have captured our imaginations from the Walt Disney Studio in a way that we never think of. Cause the Walt Disney Studio has that special magic into them from all those villains and hero's cause like they can speak for themselves like really humans.

Walt Disney has a lot of imaginations inside his mind that open our mind of hero's and villains inside the animations world. In the animations world you can open doors of any crateful characters in any way you can and that's what Walt Disney showed each and every single one of his animations. I'm admit one thing Walt Disney is a every open minded person that understand animations alright.

All of the villains are every different in there own unique way cause in really life nothing is the same if it is everything well be boring. The same thing goes with animations every villains and hero's are every different even in the animation world nothing is the same all the time if it is there is no meaning into entertaining millions of children's and adults.

My all time favorite villain that come alive is Sari Khan the tiger from The Jungle Book because he comes alive and he isn't human. Thru out the ages there's always been animals in the Walt Disney Studio and they always comes alive to me in there own characters and Sari Khan is one of them.

Mostly Sari Khan was the last villain that Walt Disney worked on because he passed on after the movie was release. Walt Disney should be every proud of himself because he bring a lathery classic alive like all of his prevented works but mostly I like Sari Khan as my favorite villain.

All of the villains and hero's come alive for millions of children's all over the world because they believe in them in a way that no one can. Cause Walt Disney put that magic into it in a way that no one can't just like me what Walt Disney done. Walt Disney put a lot of magic into my life with these characters because they can really speak for themselves in a way that no other studio can't and I'm every proud to be Walt Disney fan.

To me Walt Disney has captured my imaginations with pushing technically into a hole new meaning for somebody like me to become a writer. Even all these characters he created that can speak for themselves that's a hole lot of talent and having me have that special bond between me and my grandfather.

Chapter Twelve

The brotherhood between Walt Disney and his brother Roy Disney is no question unbreakable beside being brother they turn out to be every good friends thru out the years. Both of them were way ahead of there times about everything on animations movies you name it they done most of it. Like they always said two heads of better then one on breaking technically not afraid trying new things in life.

That shows you that anybody could be friends it doesn't matter if you are brother's or not that's what a good exploded that the Disney brothers shown. At first Walt Disney is about the name the Disney Company into the Disney Brother's Company but Roy talked him into naming it the Walt Disney Company.

Those two had a every good and special bond together almost like they don't care if they are brother's or not at long as they remand good friends. Both of them sure know how to created anything at long as you put your mind into it that's a every good advice to give anybody you can do anything at long as you put your mind into it.

Having family members working is always a good thing because you can trust the person pretty well just the Walt and his brother Roy. Like before those two know what they were doing and understating on what the people want and that's why me and my grandfather are proud to be a Disney fans.

The last thing that the both of them worked on was Pirates of the Caribbean ride in Disneyland. Both of them worked every hard on deicing the ride for millions of people could enjoy thru more then forty years because they were way ahead of there times at the time. They know by now that they well lasted a big impacted thru out the ages.

Two of them really had some magic between them beside what people think of them because they sure know how to bring something alive in animations and movies. Both of them captured millions of fans thru out the ages before and after there passing I'm every proud of there works.

Relationship between them thru out there career is fantastic they bring a hole new meaning into show business between them. Both of them bring a lot of magic thru out there careers cause they understand what the people wants in movies and animations because they take magic every seriously and equipment of the job in the Walt Disney Studio.

If both of them were alive today and see all of the technically has been broken on the Walt Disney Studio they well been blown away and proud on the legacy the both of them left behind. That's what the Walt Disney Studio is all about breaking technically to entertained millions more children's thru out the world even me growing up.

Both of them really worked well together beside being brothers I wish I could shake there hands because they made such a impacted in my life and so goes to millions of other people's life. My all time favorite thing that they every worked on is well it's pretty hard because everything they worked on are pretty good so I should say all of there work is good.

I grow up like all of there work because they really worked hard on bring good entertainment to millions of children's. Some other people might have a hard time choosing on which one is there favorite thing is about Walt Disney and his brother Roy Disney since they worked wonderfully together. Other's could choice right away on there favorite thing is about the wonderful world of Walt Disney.

Even after there passing there career well always been passed on thru other animators doing what they always loving doing and that's entertaining millions of people thru the years. Both of them knows how to find good story's and turn them into magic thru out there careers there's magic with those two working together.

My full respected to those two hard working people bring so many magic thru out the ages of animations and good movies also. Both of them are devoured there hole life's to entertained millions of people like myself and my grandfather and it was all started by a mouse by Steamboat Willie.

What they leave behind? That's a every good question Walt Disney and his brother Roy Disney left behind. Both of them left so many things to the world so they did leave something behind like the Walt Disney Studio and Disneyland all over the world. Both of them made everybody in the world believe in themselves and no wish is to big or small at long as you believe.

Walt Disney made himself believe in himself by bringing good animations to the world by one mouse name of Mickey Mouse by the 1928 cartoon short that's every bring the first to use sound called Steamboat Willie. Since then animations and sound has broken all the rules of going to the movie theaters.

Since then Walt Disney and his brother Roy Disney started something new something that no one well every dream off and hooked for life. Also Walt and Roy are the first to bring color into the world that's one of those things that the leave to behind and to bring to the world. Walt Disney Studio are usually the ones to break technically but you can't be the first to do everything in life.

Walt and Roy broke a lot of technically kind of bring a hole new meaning to the movie theaters to entertainted millions of people. Without Walt and Roy breaking new technically we wonted have the things today in motion pictures. So I would like to say thank you to Walt Disney and his brother Roy Disney for bring so many joyfulness to millions of people like me and my grandfather.

Even after his passing everybody in the Walt Disney Studio are still breaking technically like the first computer generated animation Toy Story. Without Toy Story breaking that technically no one else well never think of something like these like before never be afraid to try new things in life like Toy Story.

Chapter Thirteen

───────────── ◆ ─────────────

There is so many good animation thru out the Walt Disney Studio they always put the magic into it because it's there job it's put of the requirement of Walt Disney Studio. Without the magic the Walt Disney Studio well never come alive or anything so magic is a big part of the Walt Disney Studio.

One thing about the Walt Disney Studio animation is performance capture that one of the key things to Disney animation. For who that doesn't know what is performance capture is something that the Walt Disney Studio use since the every first live animation have been use since Snow White and the Seven Dwarfs. Performance capture is part of the magic of Walt Disney without it the animation wonted have it's animation into it.

Performance capture is the person that acts the role out for animation. The person that acts the role the animator could understand the character that they are drawing. In my opine that's a every good idea to use performance capture to understand the characters better because without it you can not understand the role that the characters are playing.

Like the early years of the golden animation they always use performance capture they always use actors to help them out. On Pinocchio the actor that played the performance capture the one who played Geppetto is the voice of that characters in history of the Walt

Disney Studio. Without the performance capture the story's well never get the help they need so it's best to use performance capture.

In the animal kingdom in the other hand they use performance capture alright they always bring animals to the studio to understand on how they draw. On The Lion King they went to the zoo because there is so many animals they have to understand on how they acted all parts of performance capture.

It doesn't matter if it's the animal kingdom or humans they always use performance capture on everything to helped them out on animations. That's how they capture our imaginations all the time with performance capture since the every first animation movie of Snow White and the Seven Dwarfs tell today's animation of the Walt Disney Studio.

My full respected to the Walt Disney animation department on everything they do on animation using performance capture on all of there hard work. All of there hard works pays off on performance captures from the passed and to the future. So performance capture are here to stay it staid back in the passed and well every be there in the future.

Sweatbox is one of things that's have been in the Walt Disney Studio since it was born there's a reason why it's called the sweatbox. First thing is that there is no air conditioner and the second reason why it's called the sweatbox is the Walt Disney himself is seating in the front and all of the employees are scared half to deaf on what he's thinking.

I wish that they had air conditioner back in those days in the sweatbox because they sure really need to cool off in the sweatbox. Now in these days they have air conditioners for everything in the studio so no one well get hot inside the studio. Sometimes I wish I was back in those days to see how they reacted when Walt Disney see thru what Walt Disney well say to the rested of the employed.

I don't know if it's not everyday having your boss check thru your stuff to see if you made any mistake on your work like Walt Disney does. That's how it's been since the every first animation movie started they always looked thru the animation inside the sweatbox.

I think that the sweatbox is a every good thing because you can see what you have done and let your boss check it out for you to see if you made any mistake. Nobody is perfected not even the animation department everybody makes mistake and you look thru your mistake and fixes it. That's why there's a sweatbox now and days to look thru your animation to see how everything is.

A idea thru out the years there always ideas because everybody needs ideas without them animation well never be there. First they need a peace of paper then they started to draw because they come more then one different version in different papers. Ideas are fun to have around because you could make good story's like that but different version in that.

Like the characters of any animation movie all of them comes different version you should never come to one ideas it comes all different ways. One character comes all different ways just not one peace of paper one character come more then one peace of paper for expulse. Cause you don't know how the character well come out as that's why there's so many ideas and different version.

Even on a sequels on a continuousness of the first story like they introduce new characters into the second film they make so many different ideas on the new characters. They always use the same characters as the first but add new characters at the same time the same old ideas and some new ones also so they could continue the story's from the first one.

Once you make a idea it comes alive something that you feel great inside on animations department in the Walt Disney Studio. You created something that comes to alive to imprecated millions of children's to captured there imaginations like no other. The creation comes to alive to open up there imaginations to free there mind to keep a open mind.

Thru out the ages in the Walt Disney Studio there's performance captures, sweatbox and the ideas inside the Walt Disney to captured our imaginations. It all started by one man name of Walt Disney and a good partnership name of Mickey Mouse on 1928 Steamboat Willie. All of the animators made hits after hits on good animation short and live action animation movie and good live action films.

Chapter Fourteen

———————◆———————

In the middle of the 1980's a new Disney company started to come called Pixar started to immerge slowly to the public eyes. It's more like computer animated the hole animation is all done by computer without any trouble but at first is done by paper and pencil everything else is done by computer.

Pixar Animation Studio is a hole another technically which makes animation something that well blow people imaginations away. Sooner or later they well have a big break on there technically bring new animation into the world and the Walt Disney Studio well be the first to have these privilege.

First big hit they got is 1995 Toy Story that the Walt Disney Studio bring to the world and it was a smash hit to the world. It's like something that no one has every seen before it's like brand new animation that bring to the world something that catch everybody off guard.

The two Toy Story films were so good that they made a ride out of it at Disneyland if Walt Disney as every seen it he well be so impressed on the effort that's going on in Disneyland. So far Walt Disney well be the first to ride on it over and over cause of the effort of Pixar effort of making a good film passing down the legacy.

Another popular Pixar movie that made into a ride is Monsters Inc since kids like monsters now and days it's just the magic into it. To me that opens up the mind to see how created on how the human mind is to created so many different monsters are inside of our mind but these is another thing kids well enjoy.

All of the characters of Toy Story are great something that no one has every thought of like all of the other Walt Disney movies there pushing technically into it for entertaining millions of children's and adults like myself. I wonted be surprise that they well push into new technically again in the Walt Disney Studio cause they always do push into new things.

My old time favorite computer animation is Cars because I use to work at a hobby store when I was young. My job was to sale toy cars to young children's toy cars and also to teach them how to build model cars it was a lot of fun and I learn so much about cars. It was a honor to work on something like that to work on a hobby store so the movie Cars brings back a lot of good members for me as when I was young.

Every Pixar movies have there own unique message about how special the movie is to them even if they have that special bond to love ones. That's why Cars means so much for me it reminds me when I was young working with toy cars. That's what I like about the Walt Disney Studio they are not afraid to push that technically into a hole new meaning.

Touchstone is a bandier for the Walt Disney Studio since the late 1980's because they are not afraid to try new things in life Touchstone is for some of the grown adults to enjoy to watch. Like the every first Touchstone film was Splash for some of the adults to enjoy watching the next step of Walt Disney.

For a fact that Touchstone is not going to replace Disney it just a new bandier so people could enjoy to watch. Touchstone made a lot of good films over the years from the Walt Disney Studio like before I would like to shake there hands on so many ideas they give to the world even on Touchstone.

Puppets are a part of the Walt Disney family because children's like myself when I was young enjoyed watching them growing up. One good movie of puppets are the Muppets Christmas Carol starting so many other puppets. Cause children's believe in them they know that they are just acting and humans control them but they believe in them like no other do.

Also for older children's they well enjoy seeing Tim Burton's The Nightmare Before Christmas. It's like a puppets version of a Halloween version of Christmas the older children's know that they just puppets acting but they don't care it's every good entertained.

Cause Tim Burton bring it to alive like no other bring things alive and the movie is every unique and wonderful.

At the Walt Disney Studio they always enjoy using puppets just like they enjoy making animation thru out the years. They always finds a way to use the magic into it and bring them alive for millions of children's all over the world. Personally you are never to old to enjoy loving puppets cause the Walt Disney puts that magic into it and it doesn't matter how old you are.

It really doesn't matter if it's drawing in paper and pencil or computer animation at long as the magic has it in there and effort into it that's all it matters. I wish that I could some of the animators cause I really grown up watching the classic Walt Disney version of his early works and even today's.

If Walt Disney was around and seen all the different movies that the animators of today have done he well be so impressed on how his legacy has still been passed on. Even at Disneyland that Walt Disney well be every much happy that there is still more people come today then before.

Chapter Fifteen

◆

One thing that live animation movies always use is a good actor or actress to do the voices of cartoon characters and it doesn't matter who it is. There is so many good talented actor and actress that do all of the good voices of the cartoon characters find the good voice is pretty hard sometimes.

Walt Disney was the original voice of Mickey Mouse which my opinion is pure geniuses because it the voice matches the character. One thing about the voices of the cartoon characters is that they have to find the good voices to matches the cartoon characters comply. The thing is the people of the Walt Disney Studio well never give up until they find the one to matches the character perfectly.

There's always one person that always been perfect that matches Donald Duck voice and that's C. Nash which is the only person that every done the voice of Donald Duck thru out the Donald Duck career. So far it doesn't matter if you are a movie star or not at long as the person is the right voice for the cartoon character that's all it matters.

Usually on sequels they use different people to do the voices sometimes but the other times they use the same person. Either ways it's still good at long as the magic is there at long as they continue what the story left off and the magic is still there in the sequel. I think it's wonderful on how hard the Walt Disney try's to find good voices on the cartoon characters.

There's a few cartoon characters that I know that never talks but remand in the Disney family for a every long time for now and forever. First character is Pluto the most beloved dog stars in the Disney family cause Pluto use body langue to see what kind of dog he is. Second person that never talks every is Dopey from Snow White and the Seven Dwarfs those are the few of the Walt Disney characters that don't talk.

One thing about doing the voices of a cartoon character is fit in with the character pretend that the character is part of you which it isn't cause there's some magic acting the role out. Playing that role isn't easy cause you don't see the cartoon acting but some times I think you do to understand the role better.

In Jungle Book 2 two of the characters of played by the same person because they have a hard time on find the other person playing that role. Which I think is doesn't matter a long as the live action animation movie is pretty good that's all it matters at long as you fit into the character. Anything is possible in animation I always believe in that cause in animation you could do anything.

You feel like the character is a part of you inside the animation if you every saw any of the classic Walt Disney animation movies never dream of doing the voice of any Disney films of today. Doing something like Walt Disney films got to have a lot of characters filling into the role believe me a lot of people enjoy working on Disney films.

You got to bring the characters alive when you are doing the voices because without bring the characters alive the story wonted have any meaning. When you are doing the voices you got to acted on the role because it's a hole lot of talent doing something like these bring the character alive.

Thru out the ages a lot of people wants to do a voice of a Disney character because they want to bring them alive just like everybody else in the Walt Disney Studio dose bring a character alive. It's like a partnership between everybody's doing without that the cartoon wonted bring any laughter into the hearts of children's.

When you are doing something like doing a voice of a cartoon character feels good cause you never know that character might be some kind of a icon thru out the world. Like Mickey Mouse has been a popular icon for more then seventy five years and we never grown out of Mickey Mouse cause true Disney fans knows that Mickey Mouse is a part of them.

Like other characters you always feel good to know that you enjoyed doing that part something you well always treasures for the rested of your life. I always wanted to do the voice of Baloo of the Jungle Book because it's my favorite movie since it's the last work of Walt Disney before his passing. Everybody has a favorite character that they wanted to do to be the voice of that character since they were a kid even me.

Being part of Disney is something that you well never replace every and you well treasurer for the rest of your life. Every since I was a little boy I always wanted to work at Walt Disney Studio it's always been a dream. Those who have privilege to work on the Walt Disney Studio should be happy to work on the Walt Disney Studio cause they are so lucky.

Even if I don't work on Walt Disney Studio I still feel like Walt Disney is still part of my life and so goes for everybody else. Also the celebrates that worked on Disney also as voices of animation movies feels the same way just not another paycheck. So everybody should be proud to work on the Walt Disney Studio or be a fan of Walt Disney.

Chapter Sixteen

Mickey Mouse is a every popular American Icon everybody seems to know since back in 1928 when he debuted in Steamboat Willie. Since then everybody is hooked to the every first cartoon that every use sound something that no one has every seen. Everybody seems to not to get enough to see everybody's favorite mouse so far everybody seems to collected everything about Mickey Mouse.

Seems like Mickey Mouse made a good impression to everybody during those times and when the years go bye Mickey started to changed. Mickey's appearance started to changed a lot but still nobody can't have enough of everybody's favorite mouse and no surprisingly that Walt was the original voice of Mickey Mouse. Everybody in America turned in to see everybody's favorite mouse ready to talk.

First words that Mickey Mouse started to say everybody got the biggest surprise in there life's but glad to see there favorite mouse in the hole wide world started to talk. It was like a world wide hit to everybody seeing something like these so far Mickey Mouse was bigger then Bugs Bunny.

Mickey Mouse played in the small screen and on the big screen that's a lot of hard work for one cartoon character but Mickey was up for the challenge for anything. For somebody like Mickey Mouse he sure bring a lot of happiness to everybody's life's Walt Disney is a geniuses when he created Mickey Mouse.

Without Mickey Mouse we well never have Snow White and the Seven Dwarfs or any other heart warming animation movies that followed Steamboat Willie back in 1928. So far Walt Disney broke all the rules ones it comes to good old animations and I'm glad what he has done he always pushing technically wants to bring new things into the world just like Steamboat Willie the every first to use sound.

The impacted that Mickey Mouse left in unbelievable the little mouse made such a impacted on so many life's to do the right thing all the time. So far everybody seems to collected everything about everybody's favorite mouse they pretty much got everything about Mickey Mouse anything you name.

For me I got a snow globe of Mickey Mouse of his seventy five birthday with some of his Disney co–stars in it to me it's every magically to have something like that. Reason why that snow globe is special because it's his birthday everybody should celebrate your birthday no matter how small or big even for somebody like Mickey Mouse.

Even somebody like me Mickey Mouse made such a impacted in my life and for future generations of people no questions about it. A lot of people collects Mickey Mouse because he's more then a mouse or cartoon character Mickey Mouse has that special magic that people could enjoy to never take advance of life and that's what Mickey Mouse is all about.

Back in the early 1980's Mickey Mouse hasn't been on the big screen for more then thirty years until everybody in the Walt Disney Studio decide to let Mickey Mouse have a come back. Like Charlie Dickens A Christmas Carol it let everybody make a guess appearance even Mickey Mouse it was nominated for a Academy Awards 1983 best animated short.

People can't have enough of Mickey Mouse because he's the best know American Icon so my best respected for Walt Disney for creating somebody like Mickey Mouse. Walt Disney created life that entertained millions of children's and adults all over the world like myself I would really like to shake Walt Disney hand.

Right now nothing bad well happen to Mickey Mouse because Mickey is the main hero for the Walt Disney Studio without him the Walt Disney Studio and Disneyland well never happen. So far there is so many reason why Mickey Mouse should stay he well never change and still remand a icon now and for the future.

From all the way from Steamboat Willie tell now Mickey Mouse well remand the biggest star thru out the Walt Disney Studio. So far nobody well every take Mickey Mouse away from the Walt Disney Studio never every. I grow up watching Mickey Mouse I feel like he's a every good friend of mine.

Chapter Seventeen

◆

Broadway always are looking for anything for a good performance out of anything and I mean anything out there even coming from a movie yes I mean movies. The Walt Disney Studio made lots of hits to bring the magic into any live action movies or live action animation movies. Going to a Broadway Theater is always good to see good shows and you never know the show you see might even come to the big screen.

There's a few live action Walt Disney animation movies that every came to a Broadway hit theater and it's pretty successful for more then ten years and that's a long time. At these days there's only a few animation that's every made it big into the Broadway hits up all the way in New York City. That's a big thing that animation made it to Broadway Theater it's every important that something like these goes untold and it didn't went untold.

One of those big hits that made it to Broadway is The Lion King the way they stayed loyal from the movie into the theater. First time it came out it was a smash hit everybody less then a second loved it how it stayed low and the make–ups and the background design it was so much really on how the theater version is.

The Lion King used some puppeteers a little bite the actors and actress are really good inside those custom's it's like you are watching really animals performing right affront of you. My favorite part is well it's pretty hard all of the show is fantastic so it makes no hard choice on tell you which is hard choice telling me which is the good part.

Second choices that become is Beauty and the Beast the only animation to nominated for Academy Award. The movie was a smash hit it has that magic because at first Walt Disney himself wants to do that personally but it was every hard so he put in the Disney Carafe to later on somebody took it. Later Head Chairman Roy Disney Jr. took it in and made it wonderful into a smash hit.

Later on the movie keeps on bring in it over and over so no surprisingly that they made it into a Broadway hit in New York City. If Walt Disney was still around and see the Broadway hit that came from the movies that he created he well be amazed like no other. The Broadway of Beauty and the Beast hit got a lot of imaginations into it and stayed loyal from the movie.

Beauty and the Beast is a timeless story it's tale as old as time nobody knows where it came from the first edition version. Nobody cares where it came from or anything all it matters the Walt Disney version has that magic into it that brings it alive. Thru out the years the Walt Disney version is much better cause since it is the first animation that every nominated for a Academy Award. Two toms up with the Walt Disney version of Beauty and the Beast on the effort they put into it.

Also no surprise that they made a ice show with all of the Walt Disney animators came to life capturing young children's imaginations. The ice show is a every good idea cause the younger generations could enjoy the new ways of Walt Disney and the young children's are lead up there faces.

One thing they always do is the background design it's every important because without it there well be no background telling you the story's all that. The color the shape and sizes is every important to see how everything moves and tell you about the background of the animals and people.

No surprise that they make remakes one of the most popular remakes is 101 Dalmatian it was remarkable wonderful something that you well never get your eye's off. The original and the remake is both every good it doesn't matter which it is the magic of it with those animals having fun working together it doesn't matter what you are outside at long as you always there to help those who needs it.

The way that the remake made those animals worked together without any trouble that's what impressed me so I really wish that I shake those guys hand on all of there hard work even the animals. I have always did enjoy watching animals working together on the Walt Disney Studio cause animals are a big part of the Walt Disney Studio for now and forever.

All around you in the Walt Disney Company there's magic into it from Broadway from all the way to New York City and here in California there's always magic inside the animation or the live action films. Walt Disney made such a impacted on everybody life's cause Walt Disney cared about entertaining millions of life's out there and it doesn't matter who you are or where you come from at long as you have a dream live for it.

Chapter Eighteen

───────◆───────

Walt Disney himself is a every nice and caring person who cares about entertained millions of children's around the world I should know I was one of those millions of children's. Always pushing technically into a hole new meaning always bringing a hole new meaning into animation and live action films.

Without them breaking technically we wonted have the movies of today or even the animations also since Steamboat Willie back in 1928 was the every first cartoon that every use sounds. That has broken technically forever and that amazed people for good knowing that they are getting something special out of Walt Disney.

I feel like Walt Disney become my every good friend since my grandfather introduce me to his work since I was a little boy. Walt Disney is part of my life I always enjoy watching his films cause Walt Disney brings them alive like no other studio does. When I was a little boy I can't waited tell school is out and come home and watch The Disney Channel cause it bring things alive for me.

A little push never hurts anybody and that's what Walt Disney did with all of his animation and movie's because he wants to bring goodness and entertainment into the world something that's every hard to do now and days. Walt Disney has the touch of believe in yourself cause you can do anything at long as you put your mind into it and I believe in that completely.

Walt Disney the live action movies and the live action animation movies were so popular Walt Disney decide to name a theme park after him named Disneyland. Inside the theme park is full of rides like no other theme park could every replace kind of feel like you are a kid in a candy store inside Disneyland.

Disneyland have the ride named after the live action animation movies some created out of Walt Disney minded watch my option is work of geniuses. Walt Disney understands what the people and young children's want inside a theme park cause Walt Disney has convinced on all of his rides. No surprise that some of Walt Disney rides become live action movies so everybody in the future well enjoy later on.

The magic with in is always importuned in the Walt Disney Studio because they take magic every seriously in all of there films it doesn't matter if it's animation movie or live action movie. Even if it's the every first computer animation called 1995 Pixar "Toy Story" there's always magic into it and the film was a smash hit to millions of children's and adults around the world.

Magic is always importuned to everything in Walt Disney and the studio thru out the ages in going to see the movies inside the theaters. Also no surprise that some of the animations become Broadway hits all the way to New York City that's been around for more then ten years. There's magic everywhere in the world of Disney thru out the years when the every first cartoon was born from Walt Disney tell today.

What did Walt Disney leave behind? Walt Disney left behind philanthropist from America to give to America he was a story writer a creator a producer he's so much in life it's hard to choice to see what he has done. Walt Disney left behind a legacy of animation followers to pick up after what he left off after his passing.

Walt Disney was a creator a story teller a geniuses for millions of world wide like myself I grow up with Walt Disney. Helping me to express my imagination to help me to become a writer to help millions of children's to read a book. Just like what Walt Disney exposure so many followers to become a animator at the Walt Disney Studio as there dream job that goes the same way on how Walt Disney helped me to become a writer.

Walt Disney death was sudden to everybody in the world like Walt Disney was like a father to everybody in the animation department. It's like somebody so close to everybody to the world has sadly gone like you loosened a every dear friend somebody that bring so many happiness to the world.

Also Walt Disney left Disneyland to millions of people could enjoy all the magic he has given to the world I should I know I'm one of those millions of children's now I'm a adult that enjoys the magic that Walt Disney has given. Walt Disney well be impressed and trilled to see how many people enjoys watching his films and followed on his foot steps to become a animator.

Thank you so much to Walt Disney that bring me the happiness in my childhood and also bring me the bond between me and my grandfather that we had to enjoy watching Disney films. So Walt Disney made such a impacted in my life so thank you again for the impacted in my life.

To the every first sound on Steamboat Willie in 1928 on the 1995 first computer animation on Pixar Toy Story the Walt Disney done everything like a normal studio to express there imagination to help express other also. Pushing technically is all what the Walt Disney Studio is doing and they are doing a wonderful job on what they are doing. Walt Disney died on December 15 1966 but his legacy well be forever be counties To Infinity And Beyond.

The End.